ELDERS

Cape Barren Island

ELDERS

WISDOM FROM AUSTRALIA'S INDIGENOUS LEADERS

Forewords by Mandawuy Yunupingu and Lowitja O'Donoghue
Photographed and recorded by Peter McConchie

CAMBRIDGE
UNIVERSITY PRESS

NOTE TO THE READER

The stories in this book were recorded circa 2001–2002. The text is a word-for-word transcription of the stories the Elders chose to tell. Headings have been added.

It is customary in Aboriginal communities not to mention the names or reproduce the images of the recently deceased. Care and discretion should be exercised when viewing this book.

Some of the interviews in this book contain information on traditional Indigenous remedies and ceremonies. Please note that the remedies and ceremonies within this book are not intended for self-use.

Map of Aboriginal Australia reproduced with permission of Aboriginal Studies Press, AIATSIS, Canberra, ACT.

PUBLISHED BY THE PRESS SYNDICATE OF THE UNIVERSITY OF CAMBRIDGE
The Pitt Building, Trumpington Street, Cambridge, United Kingdom

CAMBRIDGE UNIVERSITY PRESS
The Edinburgh Building, Cambridge CB2 2RU, UK
40 West 20th Street, New York, NY 10011–4211, USA
477 Williamstown Road, Port Melbourne, VIC 3207, Australia
Ruiz de Alarcón 13, 28014 Madrid, Spain
Dock House, The Waterfront, Cape Town 8001, South Africa

http://www.cambridge.org

© Volume copyright Peter McConchie 2003
© Text and illustrations 2003:
Chapter 1 *Healing*—Dulumunmun Maxwell C. Harrison
Chapter 2 *The Land*—Kungka Tjilpi Tjuta: Emily Austin, Eileen Brown, Eileen Crombie,
Martha Brown Edwards and Eileen Wingfield
Chapter 3 *Hunting*—Nungki Yunupingu
Chapter 4 *Gathering*—Laklak Marika [or Yunupingu] and Banygul [or Bunthami (1)] Yunupingu
Chapter 5 *Family*—Joy Wandin Murphy
Chapter 6 *Lore, Law*—Aboriginal Elders Council of Tasmania Aboriginal Corporation
Chapter 7 *Spirit*—Vilma Webb and Wayne Wonidgie Webb
Chapter 8 *The Sea*—Walter Nona and Ephraim Bani
Chapter 9 *Ceremony and Song*—George Musgrave and Tommy George

First published 2003
Printed in Australia by BPA Print Group
Typeface Baskerville (Adobe) 11.5 / 20pt. System QuarkXPress® [LS]
A catalogue record for this book is available from the British Library
National Library of Australia Cataloguing in Publication data
  Elders: wisdom from Australia's indigenous leaders.
  Includes index.
  ISBN 0 521 53924 2 paperback
  ISBN 0 521 83152 0 hardback
  1. Aborigines, Australian – Rites and ceremonies.
  2. Aborigines, Australian – Social life and customs.
  I. McConchie, Peter.
305.89915
ISBN 0521 83152 0 hardback
ISBN 0521 53924 2 paperback

CONTENTS

FOREWORDS

Aboriginal and Torres Strait Islander people are of the Land and Sea. We fit into it, we are shaped by it.

Our teaching comes from the Earth itself, by knowing the Mangrove, how deep its story, or the Eucalypt tree, where does it go down to, what level. Knowing the earth is the centre of our wisdom.

Among us there have been no written laws; our traditions are passed down through the spoken word from one generation to the next. Unity, not division, sharing rather than hoarding is our way.

So now, we write to you in your language with our timeless wisdom. Learn from us, as we have had to learn from you.

MANDAWUY YUNUPINGU

With a wonderful book like this, one wishes that it could be a thousand pages long and that Elders from every nation and every clan within Australia and the Torres Strait Islands could be listened to and their knowledge made available to all. To the Elders not included, an apology is made.

Within this book there are seventeen Elders who speak for their country. In doing so they speak about a universal knowledge that connects us and belongs to us all. These pages contain the true voice of the land and the sea.

LOWITJA O'DONOGHUE

Max Dulumunmun Harrison

CHAPTER ONE

HEALING

YUIN NATION ○ **Max Dulumunmun Harrison**

My Aboriginal name is Djarla Dulumunmun. My nation totem of the Yuin people is the Black Duck. I am a Yuin man, an Aboriginal of this land. When I think of that word reconciliation, I know it's a falseness. I know it's a lie to the people that call themselves Australians, that word has been put to the ears of these people. There can be no reconciliation between Indigenous and non-Indigenous people of this land because there has never been a partnership in the first place to reconcile about. So how can this word *reconciliation* come about and bring people together, that is the sad part. So I take this word *reconciliation* and I use it to reconcile people back to Mother Earth, so that they can walk this land together and heal one another because she's the one that gives birth to everything we see around us, everything we need to survive.

That's why people must start respecting Mother Earth for what she really is. She's not a plot that people think they can buy and own, she's not something that we can take to the grave. And we say we own it—this is crazy, this concept of ownership. I'm here to teach people let's reconcile with the Mother, with Mother Earth. If we can reconcile with the Mother, then we can breathe the air and walk together in harmony. Every part of this land is sacred: this teaching is the most important part of our survival. It's our home, we live here together. This is reconciliation, to look each other in the eye and know this equally.

KNOWING SORRY

Sorry's got to come from the spirit and heart. It will have to come from there, and the genuine concern to the atrocities of the Aboriginal people of this land. I cannot speak for and on behalf of Australians because I'm not Australian—I'm a Yuin, and no one is going to take my birthright away from me by saying I'm Australian, that's still an adopted thing to me. I can adopt other things, like being able to drive a motor car, live in a house with electricity, wear shoes, but my birthright and my naming of my birthright I will not adopt, because I would feel that I'm just adopted to this country by being an Australian. I am Yuin and I'll stay Yuin, and that's that healing thing for me there, staying true to my culture, staying true to my beliefs.

The only way I can see the non-Indigenous person making amends is by walking the land with Aboriginal people and understanding their spirituality to the land; understanding why a tree is important, why a tree is sacred; understanding why the rivers and the waters became sacred; understanding why the wind is sacred; understanding all the animals that they share this planet with.

Knowing the Aboriginal totem, if they know the totems in the area they can respect those animals, and by knowing these animals you begin to know the Aboriginal way. It's the heart-sorry and not the head-sorry that would mean a lot and heal people.

By walking hand in hand and listening to the sacred text of the land, the sacred text is every facet of the land, the story of the land, every dreaming of the land. A text is a story, a dreaming! It's the same as the text that white man brings to us in a bible, if you can put it into those Christian terms. I believe that's where something went wrong because Christianity is man-made, spirituality is god-given.

THE ROCK

I woke up from a meditation up here on the rock as Grandfather was coming up. Grandfather warming me up. I must have fell asleep all night. So I came down from my spot in the rocks and gave my thanks to the old people, spirit people. Then I thought, how long was I there? But it doesn't matter that I was there a long time, it mattered that I got answers; got healed. I was there until the third day.

THE TREE

Just through these trees we have healing through these dry bits of wood. Dry, I never said dead, because when we take that so-called dead tree and we light it, what we're doing is bringing it back to life. And when those coals are lit, or even cold and put back in the fire, and if you think they're dead, you go pick those coals out of that fire. If I asked you to, you would think I'm crazy.

OUR WORLD WITHIN THE UNIVERSE

What's there in the universe and our world within the universe? We have Mother Earth, the one that births everything for us. The food, all the material things we see around us, is what she births.

Totem Rock

Then there is Father Sky: he holds the stories of the planetary system up there, he holds the oxygen for us to breathe and also carries the water for us to drink. And Grandfather Sun, he's the old fella that grows the plants and feeds that Mother Earth that births for us; he brings out the flowers, the honeys.

Then there's Grandmother Moon. Now Grandmother Moon has got a wonderful concept of rebirthing, and birthing laws also, and she's the one that comes into the flesh woman time when Grandmother Moon goes from one-quarter, one-half, three-quarters, full moon. She's the one that can turn the ocean, lift the great expanse of waters on this planet. Man is woman first before they become men, in their mother's womb. They are woman first, so they got to start respecting the woman, because if they don't do that, how can they respect their Mother and Mother Earth. So get out of the head-stuff and get into the heart—into the spirit. Be the link in that family unit.

MEN'S AND WOMEN'S BUSINESS

Men's and women's business is also very healing to both parties. The separation of man and woman can happen because when they do there's also a union there. Learn to be respectful when they're on that separate business. That man should start thinking about that woman and her needs—the same of the children's needs. The man should then, in his men's business thing, share all that with his mates, share all that with his family males, his family men. And not to abuse the system and have that as an excuse to get away and have more men's business. That's then dodging responsibility—he'll never go home! The only time he'll want to go home is when there's sex. You see it's always good to talk out your stuff. Don't keep it in, just let it out; you never ever leave a fester, you squeeze it out, or put a leaf on it and draw it out, or you put on grass and draw it out. So the way you bring that out is by talking it out, a very good healing therapy for that male and the woman too.

Men, they got to learn to shed tears, because tears were meant to be shed and they're human after all, they're human. Men need to show emotion. After all they did it when they were a baby, they cried for food, they cried to be picked up and sung to. The man needs to do some nurturing by nurturing his family, and in return he is nurtured. Healing is so important and how we heal.

One of the dreams we can share would be how we can heal the world and how would we go about that. If we had all the world leaders in one specific place, some tranquil valley where these world leaders would be and no weapons and no fear of attack or assassination, and have some of the Aboriginal Elders to come in and talk and address these world leaders in these tranquil settings and let them take this in; and push that image there to the rest of the world, show them all the tranquillity, show them the virgin law of that land, let them be a part of it. At these great gatherings with these world leaders, they must step out of the ego and into the spirit and listen. One thing is for sure, we all breathe the same air, we all drink the same water. This is the message for everyone and to everyone!

The planet is okay—this planet will get rid of all the parasites. And the parasites are us, it's the human parasites that's causing all the destruction and not letting the planet heal. That earthquake is the planet saying look out, look out. Man has got to cleanse himself, man has got to heal himself, not with medicines but to heal himself spiritually. They must learn to heal spiritually—by bushwalking—watching the waters—listening to the wind—hear the bird sing—watching the antics of the animals, watching the birth of a flower. If we heal ourselves, then we won't have to destroy the planet, because we will be part of it.

Max Harrison, homeland

LEFT TO RIGHT: Eileen Unkari Crombie,
Eileen Kampakuta Brown, Eileen Wani Wingfield

CHAPTER TWO

THE LAND

THE KUPA PITI KUNGKA TJILPI TJUTA ○ (The Coober Pedy Women Senior Elders)

MARTHA BROWN EDWARDS

We are the Kupa Piti Kungka Tjilpi Tjuta, the senior Aboriginal Women Elders of the Coober Pedy area, South Australia. Underneath tree we make camp. If it's cold, we make it warm—fire; this tree won't get us wet, blanket, sleep. Fire close: make the fire all night, make a big fire if it's wet, then shift all the coals and sleep in the warm sand. The old people, no blanket, no mattress. This is a lifesaver to know this—this old culture before clothes and blankets.

We walked to south-west coast, no water, nothing. Middle of desert we were walking, a family, you know, going camping. Sit down, eat meat—rabbit, anything. No rifle—just dig the rabbits out, get them, or with a stick. Camp at the south-west coast, we camp, get the rabbits. It then takes five days to get to the Dog Fence from there. We sat there for a while, have a rest, because then we go and dig rabbit. We dig him out—flour, tea, sugar, that's how we grow up.

EILEEN KAMPAKUTA BROWN

We got no English but we still talking. Never mind that I don't speak English. I talk properly, talk straight. This head here got it all. I've got the knowledge. Never mind no English, don't down talk, up talk, around-the-bend talk. We talking about our Manta [Earth] all the time. I speak strong.

They don't listen. They got no ears. I've been talking on behalf of my family very strong. I can't stand up on my *tjina* [feet] very well now, but I'm still talking. My Grandmother and Mother looked after that land, that was their Manta. Now I am talking on behalf of them, so that the kids can have it behind when we leave it. My grandsons, daughters and sons.

EMILY MUNYUNGKA AUSTIN

We had a big rain, plenty of water lying around. A lot of people think we got no water out here, but we got plenty. We drink out of that sink hole in the desert, drink that nice fresh water, and that's what we're fighting for, the land. We've been everywhere—Sydney, Melbourne—we talk about our land. And they want to bring the nation's nuclear waste site here. That dump's going to affect the water, and we don't want that. We want our water. We don't want the dump here. Don't dig up uranium, leave it in the ground. It's poison to us for a long time, uranium. The old people, Grandmother, Grandfather, they told us and they know. They know it's in the ground—the Aboriginal people—know all about it. It was buried in the ground safe. Now it's all dug up, and when it rains it spreads out everywhere, and it's ruining everything.

I come from Amata, up north. That's where I was born. When the old people travelled they'd dig the water in the dry creek beds. First it would be muddy, then they would clean it out with a bowl and the water turns out clean, and we drink out of that when we travel. When they finish drinking, they bury up the soakage and leave it until next time.

The Kungkas [women] love the rain—we haven't had it for a long time, we get excited. All the Kungkas are singing out now. Big dust storm before the rain. A lot of animals rely on the water. Ducks, water hen—they all come to life and come around. Uranium's an evil thing—kill the animals. The animals drink water and it's a poison to them, and then in turn to us.

The desert, that's where they're going to bury the nuclear waste. Everyone knows it's danger, but they still won't listen. They're bringing a dump site to this land. Hey, it's going to affect all people, not just Aboriginal. Wake up, you got to wake up! The land is sacred, more than a home. We love to live in it, go out hunting, it's a free world.

Non-Indigenous people are thinking too much about money and not about being family. When Captain Cook came out, he didn't worry about the people—he just wanted the land for himself—greedy. He didn't come out here to share with Aborigines. He could have sat with us and laughed. They tried to clean out all the Aboriginals but they could not. This country is big and wide, and some of them ran away and hid away. They could never kill them all. Some people are still doing it because they bring disease, poison; they're still doing it, but sly.

Spirit fire — hand, artefact

The land was given to us, it's our home. God gave it to us, he told us to look after it and that's what we do, look after the land, and we don't like people digging it up or poisoning it. That's why we're strong, we're for the land, our home.

WARM SAND

When we were born, Grandmother cleans us with the warm sand, not with water. We'll clean by warm sand and were still doing it to this day. I was born in the Manta, born on the sand, the Earth. When belly button cord came off, we're put through the smoke. Baby wears cord around neck, keep long time until children grow up. This way baby doesn't cry.

That husband wait a long way away. Then someone will go and tell him, hey, you've got a little girl or boy. Then he'll go and get meat, go hunting. He leaves meat half-way, waits for Kunkgas to come get the meat. Only for women that place. We make a humpy to keep dry, make a windbreak, have a good sleep after the baby born. Whitefella way, sit down watch when baby born. Our way, no fella—he's making a humpy for his baby and wife. He's got to sleep opposite woman and baby on other side of fire. Father can't hold baby for long time, wait for baby to get big. Four months, five months until he can hold. Not before, not allowed to take baby, Father got to sit down and wait. Sister and brother can touch baby. No other fella allowed to hold—Father got to wait. It's the culture—Aboriginal culture big one. Whitefella come and dig up the land. Whitefella doesn't understand, they got nothing, no culture. We got sadness in the heart, we talk from the heart, not head or foot.

FIGHTING FOR CULTURE

When we walk, we got to make a camp. Our Father goes look for meat, we get a *malu* [kangaroo], then make a camp. And Grandmother, she's going to tell stories about the start of dreamtime, same as bedtime stories—she's got her stories in the heart, not on the paper. We listen to Grandmother tell the stories, then we go to sleep.

We are women who are fighting to keep the culture going. We've been teaching the younger women and the women that were taken away, teaching the people the lost culture. We really know the land. We were born on the Manta, born on the Earth. And never mind our country is in the desert, that's where we belong, in the beautiful desert country. The learning isn't written on paper as whitefellas' knowledge is. We carry it instead in our heads and we're talking from our hearts, for the land. You fellas, whitefellas, put us in the back all the time, like we've got no language for the land. But we've got the true story for the land.

EILEEN UNKARI CROMBIE

We go our own way. We know, don't touch that one, that uranium, we know it's inside the Manta, inside the ground. Then the government want to bring back the rubbish to us. No, we don't want that, we never asked for it. No, take it away, we want to keep the land for the grandchildren so they can see the country. We don't want them to kill us, we don't want the money, we want the life. We want the Manta for the grandchildren, the great-grandchildren, the little ones still coming. Our time is running out, but what about them, the little ones? It's going to be their turn to look after the land. And white man don't listen, they worry about money. We don't worry about money. We born with no money, we going back with no money, that's it. We're only here for a little while. For tea, tucker, clothing, that's good enough—not to keep money in the bank. We go back with nothing. They got to listen to us. They got to listen. We tell them a true story—no lies. We got a story in the heart. This is our story. White man got to listen— they got nothing. This one sand, it can leak through, mix up with the water. No good. We don't want them. We tell them we know there's something there before they dig it out. Old people know. They know before whitefella came for it. They told them don't touch it. Aboriginal people know it's poison.

I'm four generations. I'm two times Grandmother. You got to sit down with old people. Listen to old people if you want your life to keep going. You got to listen. Take it in. Don't just hear the word and go. Sit down, take it in—that's our life, culture.

EILEEN WANI WINGFIELD

Kungka means woman. We get along fine. We keep separate from the men. Clean this land. This is our Mother. She gives us

Eileen Kampakuta Brown

everything we need. They let off two nuclear bombs—Emu Junction in the fifties and Maralinga in the sixties.

Now they want to bring the nuclear dump here. It's too close to the underground water—that's what we don't want: That next generation are going to have a hard time with the land if the government don't pull up. What I'm saying is, Mother Nature put life here to hunt, gather, be a part of. This mining lot came in and ruin everything. We want nothing to do with this way. Mother Nature is Mother Nature. If the whitefella stands still, not blowing things up, not mining the earth, the land will stay as it is. When it's opened up, people will suffer—like they are. Whitefellas never stop and think, they're really spoilt.

We're lucky here, we've got everything. We can kill an emu, a kangaroo, whatever, and the goannas underground until summertime—you'll never find them after a big rain. So we got different food at different times. The carpet snake which we can eat, it's a big snake, longer than a person, as fat as an anaconda—lovely to eat, they not poisonous. We got porcupine [echidna] everywhere around here. In the springtime all the flowers come up, the country looks nice when they come up.

We've had a big rain, the first for a while. It feels good to the people, water everywhere.

We were living in Mabel Creek, working there in the station, the day the nuclear bomb went off. That night we went home and slept. When we got up in the morning we started getting the runs, you know, and nose and stomach trouble and everything. Our eyes were starting to get sore and sore, until they got really sore and that's why some of us went blind. Old people started passing away after that and everything was strange. Little lamb born, had three legs, no ears, and two heads. That's when I was saying, what's going on? Nobody told us—that was the trouble, everyone was hiding this. Listen to us. The desert lands are not as dry as you think! Can't the government plainly see that there is water here? Nothing can live without water. There's a big underground river here. We know the poison from the radioactive waste dump will go under the ground and leak into the water.

The government think it's in the middle of nowhere, just like it's got nothing here, but we know there is a *tjukur* [law] here all over. And we live here, and our old peoples lived here and died, and the younger generations have got to live on. And we know the *tjukur* very strong, it's all around here. That's why we talk about it, we don't want them to mess it up. Everybody thinks this country has nothing here, no sacred sites. This country is full of sites, like I said, everywhere we go there is a site for us. We keep that in our head, we don't keep it on the paper. And when it's damaged, we got to dance. We've got to do that because that's what we've got here. This is a very special place for us because we live here, we travel everywhere for our dreamtime stories and sites.

Our job is to care for the country, doesn't matter who it is, Aboriginal, non-Aboriginal. Yes, we all have to get together and look after this country because we want a clean place to live happy and healthy. When we were young, no women got breast cancer or any kind of cancer. Cancer was unheard of. And no asthma either, we were people without sickness.

When you're born in the sand, we're with the sand. And I'm one of those people, we really do care about the land. We want the Manta clean so our people can have their children this way, this is our culture! The Manta is the Earth. Stupid things are put into people's heads—you've got to go to hospital to give birth, you'll get blood poisoning, or something like that, something will set in and your baby might get sick. All around here people just have their babies, healthy babies. They're born on the warm Manta. I had three children that way.

We like to sing when we're out on the Manta, and at the end of the day we feel really good, a happy women's group. The singing the land, it gives us strength. Camp here a night or two, move to another spot. We used to do everything, work was nothing to us, out all day—get the logs back to camp and do all the artefacts, no trouble—that's the one and a big fire.

LEFT TO RIGHT: Eileen Wani Wingfield, Martha
Brown Edwards and Emily Munyungka Austin

Nungki Yunupingu — two hunting
spears and woomera in hand

CHAPTER THREE

HUNTING

GUMATJ CLAN, YOLNGU NATION ○ **Nungki Yunupingu**

I come from the Gumatj Clan of North-East Arnhem Land in the Northern Territory, Australia. There are three families that make up the clan, there's Yunupingu, Burarrwanlga and another called Mununguritj; we are all family. Our traditional homeland is Birany Birany, but I live at Dhanaya. We hunt on the earth and from it, what the earth has and walks on top of, we hunt for it; the men. We get kangaroo, wallaby, goanna, emu and buffalo if necessary; geese, especially magpie geese. The buffalo, it came in later on a boat to do the work here. The kangaroo and emu, they're the land owners here. They're Australians. Buffalo, he's immigrant; piggy-piggy, he's foreigner too.

NO. 1 ON MENU

Number one on menu is turtle, kangaroo, the red one. Turtle number one, red kangaroo entrée, then stingray when we get it. For the *gapirri* [white-tail stingray] is from November to February, in between they are plentiful. How we know is the white flowers, we call it *warrkarr* [white one] because it tells us it's stingray season. It's the start of the rainy season. What's on the land tells us what's in the water. What's going on in the forest, same things going on in the sea. When we see the rain clouds in the far west, when it's raining long way off, Darwin way or somewhere, we hear the thunder from a distance. We know stingray season is now. They come up from deep water, we look for them under mangrove roots and in shallow waters.

The manta ray hangs around the real deep waters. He's the wind maker and the man of the sea, powerful one, not for *natha* [food].

BURN-OFF

September we start to burn off the land, August, September, that's the dry season. We burn the grass and wait on the other side, where the kangaroos and all the other animals come; light the grass and forest one side, wait on the other side in a gully where there's fresh water on the river side. Kangaroo, snakes, everything, and the animals jump into the water. We burn long way off, two–three miles off, the men wait with spears. The animals think it's bushfire but lit by Yolngu men. We wait downwind, waiting when the animals, kangaroo, emu, come in, spear job. That fire also cleanses the land, through fire.

Hunters come back next day in the morning, fresh grass come up, maybe different hunters, ones that didn't come before, same clan. Different hunters, sharpshooters with spears. All the land has become cleared from the fire, so we paint ourselves with clay—animals can't smell you when painted with clay. We hunt with shovelnose spear and fighting spears, real fast ones. Fighting spear just wood with sharp end, woomera attached. A woomera can be a throwing stick to make spear go faster, can be used as a clap stick, it can be a weapon and it can be a digging stick. It's a universal tool, you can dig a ground oven for kangaroo with a woomera, use as a weapon, a club too.

EMU BIG STORY

Emu big story a lot of story. When we hunt emu, that is early job, get up way before sunrise. Walk miles to get them, we go to their favourite watering hole, that's where they used to take their bath, morning shower and all that. This was a real professional job, sharpshooters' job [with spears], real hunters that knew how to get those emu, because emu rare, rare meat, you go a long way to get them. Maybe three to five men in the tribe that were professionals, they go to dried-out creek bed or watering hole and wait.

So what they would do, still early, climb up a tree near water hole, where the emu tracks were to the water hole. Before sunrise, climb up tree. They would see them come down to the watering hole, baby chicks, mother, everything. Even kangaroos, they used to come down. The hunters were waiting up tree. The emu have two guards standing either side while the other emus go for a drink or swim; emu guards looking this way, that way, looking up, they smart.

For the hunters in the tree, everything was ready before the emu would come in—hide their faces, break the leaves off the trees for a clear shot with the spear, ready before the emu would come in to the water hole. The hunters were poised, spears ready, even before they saw them. The closest emu, the one first in the water, was on the dinner plate, he was first to get speared. Sharpshooters [with spears] so accurate they cut his neck off, that accurate.

The place where we drop emu or kangaroo, we take the guts out so he is easy to take home. We cook breakfast there, cook some liver, heart, intestines, that's breakfast. We divide up the meat between hunters. Later on, when we get home, the rest goes to the other people in the families of the clan.

PREDATOR COMING

A sign for kangaroo, where you have a certain bird they got a very loud shrill sound, they like to sit half-way down in the eucalypt. They warn the kangaroo that there's humans around, nearby. And we know that's the guardian for kangaroo, and we stop and look around; when we see the bird, we know there's kangaroo. It's the female kangaroo that you got to be careful about, she's in the bushes looking about. She doesn't go to sleep, only the husband goes to sleep in the daytime; the female near just eating, sitting and looking. When she hears the bird she goes thump, thump, thump with the tail, to warn the others there's a predator coming.

SIGN LANGUAGE

Just sign language when hunting, or whistle in code, same as bird. No talking, you have to be quiet, sign language. That is hunting the kangaroo. For the turtle you have to be quiet as well, in the dugout canoe same language for hunting.

COURAGE

All the animals would go into the holes, any holes, even the animals that hate each other like the goanna, the lizard and the snake, all go into the one hole when there's a fire. 'Come on, come on, let's go in the hole.' They got to get away from the fire.

After fire the Yolngu come in and reach down and feel their skins. If it's a smooth skin, they know it's a snake; if it's rough, that's the goanna. They pull him out, dangerous all right. The Taipan or the King Brown, when they feel Yolngu they sort of go up the Yolngu arm, sniff, sniff, sniff. They stop middle of arm first, then they stop at the neck of the Yolngu. It takes a person of real courage to do this. Don't pull your hand away or you're finished, or when they come to your neck and sniff don't turn your head or it would be bad luck.

Nungki Yunupingu hunting turtle

Snakes will be first out of the hole. They know fire has passed away because Yolngu is there. You can almost hear their breathing when they're at your neck and stop when they leave the hole. It took people of courage to hunt this way, there would be one, two, three, four goannas down there, enough to feed the whole family, maybe even more goannas and even more snakes sometimes.

KING BROWN

Sometimes they get fierce and chase you, and they travel faster than you. We must climb the tree to escape. They can't climb the tree; they try, but they can't. They will sit there until you drop from exhaustion, all night they wait for you there, they don't go anywhere. King Browns wait all night, maybe all the next day, they wait to kill you. They're shy because they have been interrupted mating or something, anyone interrupt them they're finished, they just chase you. Either light a fire, throw it to the ground to get rid of them, or get a stick from the tree, put your sweat from armpit on the end and let them sniff it, they go, they know it's Yolngu.

NGAPAKI

Fish is everyday *natha* [food]. It's not hard to go hunting for, relaxing. But turtle we have to go long way out, same as dugong, go where turtle is plentiful. Where there is seagrass, the turtle and dugong are. Dugong has small ears but it can hear you from a mile away, when you hear them, *yakka* [no] noise, don't make any noise. That's where the sign language comes in.

TURTLE HUNT

Traditionally the boats were cut from paperbark trees, the whole tree. They get huge, real big. We get them from swamp area or forest. The turtle goes to feed when the tide is coming in; it feeds on the seagrass in shallow water. The hunter before harpoon time would jump on the turtle, grab on the tip of the flippers, then they got no power to run, another couple of hunters get in the water drag him up. If the turtle was too big, they tip the boat, put the turtle in the boat and bail the water out, then take him home alive, then kill. Meat stays fresh, we cook in ground oven. Whose area the turtle would be taken from, some of the meat would go to the land owner, from where that turtle would be caught from, a good piece. Or even for a person we would borrow a harpoon from, or the owner of a boat, we feed him well with the meat given.

TRAPPING FISH

At night-time the tide comes in. When tide goes out it leaves pools of water with the fish trapped inside. May, June, July, August to September, five months of fishing here in the same area. We put rocks there, around the edges, to make it harder for the fish to escape. We even find sea turtle trapped in there. Sometimes the eagles try to get them, but we chase them away. We get up early to beat the eagles, at times we camp there and get them early. These fish traps would feed us all, but right tide and right season. Low tide in the morning no worries; even dingoes walk into the pools chasing fish.

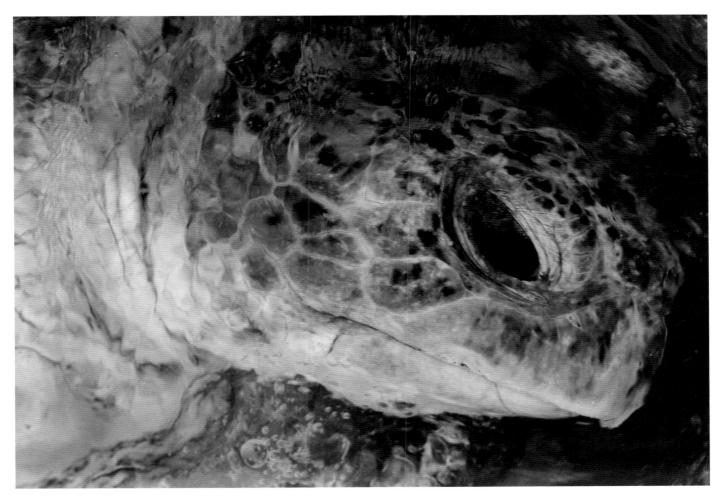

Old Turtle

Bunthami (1) Yunupingu

CHAPTER FOUR

GATHERING

RIRRATJINGU CLAN, YOLNGU NATION ○ **Laklak Marika and Bunthami (1) Yunupingu**

We are Elders for the Rirratjingu Clan, male Elders gone. We Elders for Yalangbara, Yirrkala and this island. This island is our home; its Yolngu name is Dhambaliya. We came here to get away from the negative side of Ngapaki [non-Indigenous] culture: our real homeland is Yalangbara. We were the ones who grew up the children here, going out gathering bush foods, feeding them with everything the island provides. We go out in the morning and stay out all day. Gathering is women's job. We take the children, boys and girls. When boys at seven to eight begin to make spears, they stay behind at the camp, begin to distance themselves from the women. When the boys are ten or eleven, then they go with the men for learning. The Mother takes the children; when they newborn she has to carry them. Crawling, beginning to stand up, walk, onwards from the start of life they come with us.

Laklak Marika

CALENDAR PLANTS

While we are gathering *dhan'pala* [mud mussels] we are teaching the young ones the right food to collect, what season to collect, educating about the wild fruits, looking at seasons for foods by looking at plants. 'See that plant, that tells us we got good honey season coming up.' Nature telling stories, and we're connected to these natural stories. We don't write it down and give to the kids; we teach through talking, telling and showing. That's Yolngu way.

MEDICINE PLANTS

No shop here, we collect food for our grandchildren and children. When we first moved to this island it was very hard time, but still we learnt our way, we went out and looked for it! No boat, no airstrip for plane, no anything.

We feel strength and power from this food. Shop food just to fill up stomach, that's all, true; just to fill up stomach. Bush food has no sugar, we can walk a long time with this. When our people get sick, we feed them bush food to heal. Us old ladies gather medicine plants when someone's sick. What's for boil, what's for eye, what leaves to get, fruit for sickness. We know how to prepare for that person, medicine for backache, boils, sores, eye, headache. Our natural medicine doesn't cover the problem, it cures problem. Before Ngapaki, no cancers, leprosy, HIV, chickenpox, none of it. It came from changing the environment.

CYCAD DAMPER

Seeds from the cycad start off green; then when yellow, is ripe, ready to take out poison and prepare for food. Put into bag called *gay'wu* [collecting bag], dig a hole where the water running, put there, cover with sand. Wait five to six days until poison gone, grind up seeds, make damper. Is for anytime, cycad damper, or for big ceremony, cleansing ceremony, circumcision. Find that one inland, not on island home; cook in earth oven. Good for eating while walking long distance too, you can keep this bread for months before eating.

We collect gull eggs. Used to go by canoe to the little islands, that's where the gulls like to lay their eggs, but by canoe long time ago. There is a special grass that grows that tells us when the gulls lay eggs. When the head of the grass goes brown, that's the time to go!

Managing the land is natural way for Yolngu. We know when to take, when to leave, so always plenty for later. We have good

Yams in front of fire

relationship with land, we know the seasons. There is a lot of food for Yolngu on this island.

Men hunt big meat, turtle, kangaroo, emu; Women, oyster and clam meat, mud crab, mud mussels. Cook the mussels in the coals, they got their own pot and lid, the shell with the meat inside! Our way is universal way.

Joy Wandin Murphy

CHAPTER FIVE

FAMILY

WURUNDJERI ○ **Joy Wandin Murphy**

Healesville, Victoria, is where my Father was born in 1896. Healesville is white man's name for this part of Wurundjeri land. This is part of my Father's country. He was a senior man to my Mum, twenty years older than my Mum; he was the youngest of four brothers and five sisters. His traditional name is Jarlo Wandoon, he was an Elder of the Wurundjeri people.

My Mother was not chosen for my Father. The time they came together was after the Half-Caste Act. White man had been here for some time, traditional family ways had been taken away from the Wurundjeri. My Mum was reunited with her Mother at the age of seventy. We found out that her family was from Warrnambool on the Victorian [west] coast; they are called the Gunditchjmara. But Mum was born in Sydney and, after she was separated from her Mum at the age of three, travelled a lot with her foster parents. Her foster father was a man of the cloth. He became a minister because that meant his family would be protected because Indigenous children were head-counted—the government knew how many kids were in any one family at any one time. And the way that my Mum became a part of their family was that, sadly and tragically, they had lost a little girl who was also a three-year-old. And when they came across my Mum and her Mum, my Grandmother was going to end Mum's life and hers by jumping into a river in Sydney. They offered to take my Mum from my Grandmother, because they had just lost their little girl.

There was this gap in their family and my Mum was much the same age, and they said there would be no questions asked by the authorities because they had the same amount of heads. My Grandmother was going to jump from the bridge with my Mum because my Grandmother's three-month-old son was taken from her arms and she only had two children, and she wasn't going to let the authorities take her only other child. So my Mum travelled with what was called her foster family. She came here, ended up here.

CORANDERRK

The Half-Caste Act was after the Aboriginal Protection Board was set up, so that Aboriginal people were seen to be protected, but really controlled, by the government. But what the intent was, was that Aboriginal people would be totally assimilated. Around the 1850s, mid-50s to 1863 when Coranderrk was first established, a place was needed to pull all the Aboriginal people together so they could manage and control them. So this is why the government thought they couldn't have us wandering around just aimlessly. We were put all in one spot like cattle, a herd of cattle, to manage us. It was originally 4850 acres; it was the only permanently gazetted land in Victoria. The land was supposedly never to be revoked by an act of parliament, but in less than sixty years, from 1863 to 1923, from 4850 acres it was reduced to half an acre, which is now Coranderrk Aboriginal Cemetery.

In the early 1880s Coranderrk became totally self-sufficient running their own school, cattle, milking their own cows, making their own bread, gold medal prize-winning hops, and making bricks. The government said, this is just not on. Aborigines self-determining and managing their own affairs.

They had to find a way to close Coranderrk Station.

The tribal language was not allowed to be spoken. And my Granny was one who said they would not stop them speaking language. She was a leader and hoarded all the women together in her house and they would sit around and talk language. The men had a harder time with this; they were stalked and not given much free time together.

Over time, despite restrictions on us, they decided—because Aboriginal people were prospering and not dying off and not wasting away—the government then decided to do something else to break this down. So the 1886 Act came about, and they classed it as the Half-Caste Act. It was a criteria set that anyone who was seen to be half-caste—that is, black or white mix of blood—who was of an age, and they put it at age thirty-five years, must leave the reserve. Which meant able-bodied people who were able to work, who were able to help keep our people's strength, were removed from this place, and this was part of the assimilation process to wipe out the Aboriginal race.

So that was in 1886 when able-bodied men were sent away. By the early 1900s Coranderrk was really falling down, so badly a lot of people became sick. A lot of the Aboriginal women met up with white men and moved away. The government served their purpose with this Act. And then by 1923 there was nothing. They said all people should leave Coranderrk. People refused to leave, and one was Granny Lizzy Davis and the other was a man by the name of Dan Russell. Eventually they were granted permission to live there.

BEFORE INVASION

My Father, as the youngest of ten, had seen a lot of things happen in a short time. In his life he had gone through traditional to contemporary ways in a relatively short time. He was only twenty-one when he went to war. So for the first fifteen years of his life, it changed dramatically. It was not about cutting a canoe out of a tree, it was not about making a boomerang from the roots of a tree. It stopped being about catching an animal for tucker, or fish for tucker, or any of that. It was about bringing cattle to Coranderrk, this strange animal he had to learn about—food brought into the area, and on top of this growing from a boy to a man overnight. And that's why he was so earnest about going to war to fight for his country, his

Eagle

people, and to give them identity and to hopefully give them some rights in this place. My Dad was about 5 foot 8, he wasn't the tallest of his mob but he had a very strong demeanour. He knew what he needed to do and he was going to do it.

What you had to do back then to enlist was get to Melbourne, so he walked there—didn't have a car or anything—and signed up. On the papers it had what nationality you were, like it did on most papers, and he put Australian Aborigine. This was in 1918, and he was rejected from the Australian army and came home. He was adamant he was going to fight for his country and change things by recognition being given to Aboriginal people. The only way he could legally be accepted was to sign up as a black American, and so he did. And in 1919 he did two years overseas and came home with medals. The other soldiers knew he was an Aboriginal, they all knew who each other were, they were mates, they were all mates. My Father was in the signal corps.

After the war nothing changed for Aboriginal rights. His army mates could not believe how badly treated he was when he returned to Australia. His whitefella mates said how ridiculous this was. They fought over there for the same reason, for Australia, to keep it free for people.

SURVIVAL

In traditional times there was the man who had responsibilities, such as going out and getting the big game meat, going ahead looking for a camp, preparing it. The women would be the gatherers of food, nuts and the berries. Birth is women's business. They have that sole responsibility to make any decision with their children, but they would also have a huge responsibility with their child or children, with all they had to do, with the gatherings they had. If it was too much to carry and if there was a sister or auntie or someone else to carry that child, then that child would be okay. If the child was ailing or sick, to the extent they would have to stop what they were doing for survival to tend to the child, meant they would fall behind their party. And at times the women would have to make a choice to end that child's life. This was not done matter-of-factly. It was such a strong position between mother and child and having that sole responsibility, so much. The man would never question the Mother; he knew it wasn't his business to ask, and that she would make the right decision on the behalf of the child and the family, and it was about survival. Sadly, if this child was too ill to go on, then a decision would have to be made. And the Mother would have to kill the child literally, rather than leave the child for some animal to come along and maul it to death which would be totally improper, or wait with the child until time of passing. It wasn't like picking up the phone to the doctor and saying I have a sick child. It was their culture, their tradition. That was the way they dealt with things; they were the only people there to deal with the situation.

The land lays out family law by telling you what should happen. The land doesn't dictate to the family, but rather guides with the knowing of what the land means to the family—how to be with it, what comes from it. There's always the sense about instinct and if that instinct isn't followed, you go astray, the family can suffer.

Traditionally we didn't celebrate birthdays, nor the silver anniversary for husband and wife. You were born and not measured by years. It wasn't about how long you were married, but who you were in that family unit—Mother, Father, children, Grandfather, Grandmother, Auntie, Uncle. Our celebration was about living; age was about wisdom and knowledge, not how old you were.

STOLEN GENERATIONS

Many children were taken from their families. To my knowledge, none of my Uncles or Aunts were taken away from their Mums. And yet my Grandmother, the mother of ten children, which includes my Father, she was brought down from Echuca supposedly as an orphaned child. But we know she wasn't an orphaned child, more likely a child removed from her family.

Division, the government wanted to divide the family. What was behind that is that they saw us as savages, as not human beings, and that we were not able to look after our children properly, that was the mentality of the colonial-minded people. They must have known in their own heart how they would feel if their own kid was taken away, and why did they do it the so-called religious way, hiding behind the sacred cross.

If you think about the holocaust, it was a government order. This is white man versus black man in our case, two totally different people, two totally different cultures, treat us like slaves, so we're disciplined the colonial way. Take everything out of us, heart, spirit, and take out the soul; hollow us out, fill us up with new unknown and bad stuff. People ask me how can you deal with the churches with what you do, but I say I want them to know what culture is from an Aboriginal perspective, but I can't do that if they are my enemy.

I am a boorai *[child] of this land*
My old ones tell me my spirit
Belongs here
I walk on this land like no other
Following my dreaming tracks.

Jim Everett, Cape Barren Island

CHAPTER SIX

LORE, LAW

PLANGERMAIRREENNER CLAN, BEN LOMOND TRIBE ○ Jim Pura-lia Meenamatla Everett

My name is Jim Pura-lia Meenamatla Everett. I was born at Whitemark, Flinders Island, off the north-east coast of Tasmania. I am from the Plangermairreenner clan, of the Ben Lomond tribe, north-eastern Tasmania. There are nine tribes made up of various numbers of clans covering Tasmania. Ben Lomond, our mob, had three clans. We can have a tribe with up to fifteen clans and different dialects for almost every clan, that was the make-up we had.

Contact with the other clans was not always good. Fighting over things, like stealing of women, as you couldn't marry back in your own tribe, and you couldn't always get an arranged marriage. The men who needed wives would go and steal, and the other mob would come back and retaliate, to the point where people were killed. They would all do it; the tribes needed more children, otherwise the tribe begins to deplete. It's about keeping the balance of numbers of people to keep the clan going, so you do what you've got to do.

If somebody crossed into someone else's cultural boundary without approval, to hunt or pass through, this could cause conflict, without asking for permission. The law is to sit and wait at that land boundary. Sit and wait, and after a while the right person would come out and talk with you to see what your business was. If they were happy they would bring you in. The same protocol existed between all the Aboriginal people.

THE LAW OF THE LAND

We never fought over ground, we never fought over territory. The land had created the boundaries, not us. The Law of the Land and our responsibilities, they were laid down by the land itself. Aborigines have never ever tried to change those cultural land boundaries. That was the Law of the Land, and there is the responsibility of each of the groups to the land where they lived.

Being responsible citizens of our Earth Mother means we have to be responsible to the other citizens of Earth Mother. This means the possums, kangaroos, the bird, the fish; we look after their environment, and they look after us. If you don't show due respect to the water, the water gets sick; your Sister Water is then no good to you or anything else. You formed a responsibility to your Sister Water, that fellow citizen that you should be showing respect to, not to see yourself as superior to her.

The reason we are here is because of the lands, and the lands' rights; so we got to understand—all of us, no matter what culture—that the land has rights. We, the Tasmanian Aboriginals, are a people fighting our way back from extinction.

The big challenge to Aborigines is to live in the modern world and embrace the Law of the Land. Originally, all people came from societies that were Indigenous, and then technologies developed. As part of our responsibility to our land we must reconnect all people back to their original responsibility to the land—this Law belongs to all.

LORE

Lore is the Rules of the Land, the life on that land. That might not only be animal life, that may be the trees, plants, water and so forth. So these things have particular behaviours and those behaviours are meaningful because they have been set by the ecology of this planet, and people who connect with that fit into the Lore of the Land, which is the basis of all our survival.

If white Australia can reconcile itself to the land and understand the Lore of this Land and the reason why this land is the way it is, that will be a great part of conciliation. Aborigines don't need assimilating. We can choose it if we want to, but we've got to be given back the resources that we need to live a cultural life in a modern world without being told by the government how to do it.

THE LIE

At the time of colonising Australia, a place that was said to have no living inhabitants, that had no government, that land was considered *terra nullius*. *Terra nullius* is a self-serving definition made by the nations that were in the business of colonising in the 1500s, 1600s and 1700s.

There were a number of definitions for *terra nullius*. The use of the word here in Tasmania was on unoccupied land, meaning that the people who were from there didn't have government, agriculture and so forth, and therefore were considered to be like animals running around feeding off the land. And therefore we were considered to have no so-called real purpose, because it was not thought to be civilised to be eating off the land. You've got to rip it apart, tear the heart out of it, cut all the trees down, build roads and houses, pollute and change the waterways, and then you can say you're civilised; and we, the Aboriginal people, didn't do that, and so we weren't civilised.

Then Australia's own High Court threw out *terra nullius*, as it was recognised as being a lie by its own government. To this day we're still living under white Australian law, which is an illegal law over this land. White Australian law says it's okay to rip open the heart of the Earth Mother and take all the minerals, and it's all right to cut all the trees down, to dump rubbish and pollute the sea, take all the fish from the sea. It's all right to dump nuclear waste without considering future generations, because whitefella's law says you can do it—that's the difference. Their laws are about possession and control. In Tasmania, we have been given back thirteen parcels of land, amassing a total of less than 1 per cent of the total area of Tasmania.

Non-Indigenous Australia is made up of a mixed racial origin of people that call themselves Australians. However, mixed-racial-origin Aboriginal people are immediately called half-caste, quarter-caste, part-Aboriginal, etc., but not called Aborigines. Society's rules have been set.

Aboriginal people have been through a number of structures politically. We've had the Department of Native Affairs, Department of Aboriginal Affairs, the Aboriginal Development Commission and now the Aboriginal and Torres Strait Islander Commission—ATSIC.

These organisations have been moulded into the administration of government to implement the government's policies down into the Aboriginal communities. They do not come and sit with the Elders and find out what we want and hear our voice. It's all policy down from the government. These political Aboriginal organisations are silent on the environment issues of this country, about the destruction to our lands and waters—these so-called leaders are lost. But they have been bought; the land and sea would not be suffering if they were true to our culture. If we think we need white man's money to develop our culture into our communities, then we ought to throw our culture away, because we've lost if we need money to keep culture alive!

Cape Barren Island

Vilma Webb

CHAPTER SEVEN

SPIRIT

WA-DANDI AND BIBBULMAN CLANS, NOONGAR PEOPLE ○ **Vilma Webb**

The people from down south believe when their people died, they went out through the limestone caves, went out across the horizon to the resting place and with the old man of the sea. His name was Wardan Corinup. And that's what a lot of those people believe. We are spirits from that place because we're living down here and we're Wa-dandi people. Wa-dandi people and that, they think we came down from the caves. They think we're already dead, that we're from the spirit world, and that's why they're frightened of us. If we go up the country people won't talk to us. They turn their back on us anywhere we go, they will turn their back on us, not talk to us, because they're afraid of us.

MASSACRES

I know when the lands had massacres. I could feel them when I go in there. And if they don't want me to go to certain places, they won't let me go there, but I can sit down, talk to them, and tell them who I am and what I'm doing there—then they'll let me go past. That's like I was saying, if they don't want you to go past they will stop you and pull you back down. If they want to come with you, they jump into people and take over. Sometimes when they want to come with you out of these areas they'll do that, and they get to where they want to go and then they leave you.

WONIDGIE, WAYNE WEBB

My name is Wonidgie, my name means Speaker of the Dead. My Mother's land and Father's country is my homeland. That country goes right down to the most western point in Australia, which is Cape Leeuwin. Mum's takes in all the south country and Dad's takes in all the north-west country up to 50 kilometres south of Perth. That's my homeland right through.

When my Father passed over, his responsibilities were passed on to me. Before, I would say, 'Go and ask him and then come and see me', but now I speak for the Wa-dandi side, my Father's land, and also for Bibbulman side, my Mother's side. My Father passed away on Easter Sunday. Two weeks before that he took us to the spot he wanted to be buried, my wife and myself. When he did pass over, we buried him two weeks after that—which gave all the people throughout the country a chance to come. Six hundred people came, three hundred black, three hundred white. We buried him in his own country, up in the Busselton, Margaret River area. We buried him there in his country in the traditional way in the bush. The Noongar sat their people up in the grave facing the east, so that when the sun comes up in the morning it warms the spirit, the people, always see the sun coming up in the morning and placed where the sun's going to shine at the end of the day on the person.

We wrap food in the paperbark, and anything the family want them to take on their journey into the next life—whatever they are going to be created as. We believe that when people are going to be recreated they come back as something of the earth. The earth is our Mother and we always come back to her. We're only here for a short time and have to work with her, look after her, not abuse her in any way, because we'll always go back to her. And she'll look after him now that he has travelled on to the next life and he will come back as a person, a bird or an animal, a kangaroo even a tree, anything that's got to do with the earth which is the Mother. When you're born, you're part of your Mother; you don't fight against that.

SORRY TIME

When a person passes over, we do a smoking, a small fire, let the smoke drift across the body to safeguard the spirit on its journey. At the time of Dad's passing over, we buried him the old way that night. When we went home, my wife and I stayed at Mum and Dad's place, and we had a little dog on the bed. We've had that dog for years. During the night my wife and I woke to the dog laughing and it was my Father's laugh. This lasted about ten minutes. We just let him go. He was having a good time, my Dad, his spirit was coming through our little dog. He laughed so clearly, he was happy and on his way.

Old people know when they're going to pass over. They visit the family to prepare to say good-bye. Sorry time can last anything from a week to a couple of months, to twelve months, right through until the things around have been put away, photos, personal belongings. And then the people come back out and settle back into their lives. In a way it's sorry time, but we know they're on a journey. It's also a happy time, a time of recreation.

There is a difference between Indigenous and non-Indigenous people spiritually. White people seem to be set on driving a materialistic way of life. There's a few Indigenous people going the same way, those that have lost touch with what they're here for and the meaning of why they're here living the white man's way. 'Have a look at my new stereo', 'I own a car'—owning new things, replacing them with newer models, existing to prop up a cycle void of spirit—a world full of distractions. In our culture if someone likes something you're making or have, you often give it to them. Spiritual beliefs are the foundations of our culture—material without true spirituality is without foundation, eventually it will collapse.

When someone passes on, the spirit comes and lets the ones closest know they come and visit during the night. Sometimes we get a death rain, a light drizzle of rain that lasts all day. Our people believe that they go in threes, our belief that they go to keep each other company in the next world life. We wait and ask who's going to go next, and sure enough they do!

Wonidgie in ancient forest

SPIRIT AT HEART

We're only here for a short amount of time to do what we've been put here to do, which is look after the country. We're only a tool in the cycle of things. It takes two people to make a baby, and that baby is nurtured by the Mother until it is able to go out into the world and help and keep the balance of nature. It's a big cycle of living with the land, and then eventually going back to it and recreating something new.

Most of the forest around here and in our country has got hollow trees that have been burnt out. We believe that the hollows of these trees hold our people, the old people that have passed on. If you're in the forest late at night, that's when the Mumari or the Woodachi wander around looking for a person to go into. Half an hour before sunset you get out of these areas and home and get away from the forces of these spirits. Whenever I leave an area I pick up everything, even my hair if it catches on a tree; I leave no hair for spirits to follow me home. The connection between you and what you leave behind in the bush, you can get followed home. And when we leave, we always draw a line behind us so the spirits won't cross that line and follow us home. If you stay too long, the old spirits begin to smell on your body.

On Noongar land, if we walk into an area with spirits we feel them both in and around us. They're there watching us on an old massacre or burial site. It could be the hottest day in summer and we feel the chill of their presence. If we feel the bad spirits we get out, it's not right. Other times it's just the chill but we acknowledge the presence. There's a lot out there in that spirit world. If the white people understood and respected the world this way, it would be a very different place.

When someone passes over, we don't use their name; we say Coomidah. If someone's name is Bill, they won't use that; they call him Coomidah. We respect their spirit. On Noongar land there are many languages and the ones that travelled had words that were understood by all the tribal lands.

NINGARRANA, THE DEVIL

A giant devil, the story is he eats the children and older people. Most of the Noongar know these stories. The people head home before dark, they won't be out after sundown, because we believe that Ningarrana and all the spirits move around at night. A true story, part of our dreaming; it keeps the clan together and close together. We always knew the people were okay because they would come home. The kids, everyone, we wouldn't have to go looking for the kids after sunset because of the stories they are told. They knew to get home, it's instilled in them, in their spirit and in our stories, Ningarrana's still around.

TOTEM

In southern Western Australia, this area here, we had a lot done to us, with murders and rapes—things like poisoning water holes, massacres. The people that were killed, their spirits are still wandering here. When a person is killed, their totem can't be used as a food source by anyone. Communities starve rather than eat a friend or a family member's totem; it would be like eating them. If they were to eat the kangaroo, it would be like eating their brother or sister. The time of abstinence can last between six and twelve months. Different tribes, different beliefs. My totem is the kangaroo, I don't eat kangaroo.

Before the early settlers set up in Walpole, the sealers and whalers from America were travelling the coast, travelling between Albany and Perth, always coming past. They would stop and take women from the tribes for months, rape them and throw them overboard or drop them off on someone else's country. And you're not supposed to be in someone else's country, they'd get speared, killed. Or if they did get back to their tribal group, they were outcasts—run her out of the tribe, she may have brought a sickness back from that time with the sealers and it would wipe out her tribe. The raping and murdering was going on then, and it accelerated when settlement began. This treatment is still going on now but in a different form. The government still got to play games, just with a new set of rules.

MURDER

The Europeans thought of us as just Neanderthals and barbaric. As far as we were concerned, the Europeans were the barbaric ones. What gives another the right to kill just because they want that bit of land you're living on. In Dad's country there were three hundred people killed there. One settler went and took the leader of the clan Gaware's wife as his own. This early settler wouldn't give his wife back, so Gaware speared him in the chest. Now they knew exactly who Gaware was and what he looked like, all about him, but they just went out and killed everyone—women, children, warriors, everyone, whoever they saw. They killed them in the rivers and buried them in the sand dunes, in caves and hills up in my Father's country.

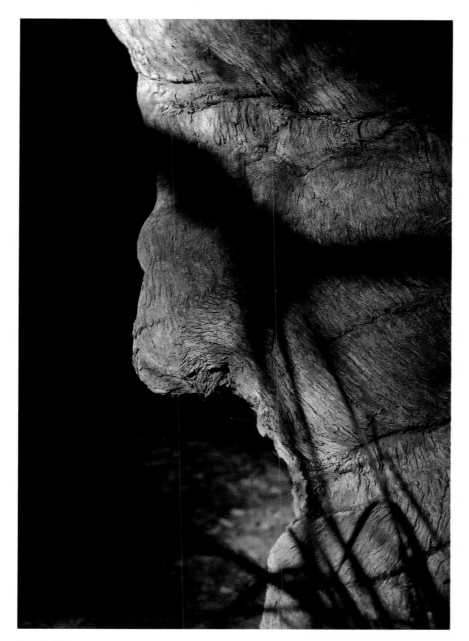

Tree Spirit

My Great-Great-Great-Grandmother witnessed what happened and passed on the story. They did things like burying babies up to their necks in the sand and see who could kick the head of the baby the furthest, riding people down and running sabres or swords through them. So we had all of this done to us, our spirit and people. We retaliated to save our women and our people from being wiped out! They were classed as heroes, those whitefellas for what they went out and did.

All the people that are creating the destruction don't have a feel for the land, for the environment. They're not connected, there is no belief. They believe the Prime Minister or the Queen, but the Indigenous people listen to Elders. We don't vote someone in, ours is natural leadership, natural born. It comes through how they speak and direct people in spiritual things, leading the people through different issues. They're not appointed, someone just takes the role.

SPIRIT JOURNEY

Seeing into the future, not just astral travelling but dreaming, go on a journey in dreamtime, a chance to look into the future.

The old people would travel this way often and advise the rest of the tribe, as a visionary of the tribe. All people are spiritual—there is no one between you and your God. Aboriginal people believe in a similar creation story. Although the people all over the country have different names and different stories for their beliefs, it's all similar.

THE REDTAIL COCKATOO AND THE OWL

The redtail cockatoo, he's special to our people and I think a lot of mobs around the country—the old doctor men, people call them Bulya men or Mabarn men. Around here they were the old blokes that carried out the lore made by the Elders and we believe they could shape-change to what they want. They were the ones to go out and punish the bad ones who break the lore. That's why the redtail cockatoos sometimes travel in threes: it's those old men travelling to carry out the wishes of the Elders. And when the old Mabarn men would do the doctoring, they would shape-change into the owl when someone was sick. We call them lore keepers and are courteous if we see them. If you had done something wrong, then you would be fearful, reason is they'd be coming for you.

Walter Nona

CHAPTER EIGHT

THE SEA

THE TORRES STRAIT ISLANDS ○ Athe [Great-Grandfather] Walter Nona

I am praying for all the Indigenous people and all the white people too, because we are one. We are all one family, all brothers and sisters. My responsibility as an Elder is to pass knowledge from one generation to the other, and make sure this knowledge is correct.

My personal totem is the snake. When it is time to die, all the actions of the snake come to us, the eyes become glassy. We act like the totem at this time of passing—the stingray, the crocodile, whichever totem belongs to the person. The last action the person makes before they die is those movements of their totem. The sea is where we get all our food from; those reefs around the islands of the Torres Strait are our fence. Even the reef along the Queensland coast, that's the fence for our

Aboriginal brothers and sisters too! When we fight for our own sea rights, we fight for our Aboriginal brothers and sisters too! The sea is our highway between the islands.

Our ancestors travelled by canoe using only paddles, sometimes twenty people in a single boat. Each tribe makes the canoe their own way, they keep these canoe-building secrets to themselves. Sometimes the trees or the hull would come from Papua New Guinea—much was traded. Some things needed to be traded between the islands, the sea was our highway to allow us to travel.

BEFORE HUNTING

Before you go hunting you've got to talk in language, ask permission. You ask permission from the spirits to guide you. The spirits will be there with you and they can get the dugong and turtles that are closest to you to come to you, so you don't have to travel much, just go get your catch and come back. If you don't ask permission, you get nothing. The weather is told to us by the moon and the stars as well. The moon, stars and clouds tell me in signs. No matter where you are—inland, away from the sea, it doesn't matter. I can tell the types of tides by the stars too. When I go hunting, I give something that is with me to the sea—drinking water I give to the sea, some food I give, that's in our culture. That's how you get everything easy for you—because you ask the sea for permission again. If you don't ask, you won't get. You have got to treat the sea with respect.

If I go hunting and see a shark come from one side and then across my dinghy, I know something will happen from that direction; if shark came from the other side, I know the meaning to this too. I know first before I am told—the sea shows me the sign, it is very clear!

Bamboo means life in our culture. If you see that bamboo grow wrong you got to straighten it up, so it grows straight. Once it is bent and dry, you can never straighten it up. There are many bamboos. You can't just cut any bamboo for a spear, it's got to be the right type. That spear you will end up making will reflect you, you make it to reflect you, and part of you is in that spear, and you take care of it. You treat your spear with respect.

When the bamboo is young, it's soft like our children. You got to teach them better ways—when the bamboo is old and dry

you won't straighten it: Doesn't matter how you try to change
your kids when they're older. When they're young, you teach
them what's right from when they're young.

SHARK

When we see the shark jump or the stingray jump, doesn't
matter if the sea is calm, we know it's going to become rough
because the shark and the stingray know this by the sea inside.
Or if the seafloor is rolling, we know it's going to be rough, so
when we finish our business there, we move on. It's going to be
rough when the seafloor does this! Then we know to work our
way back to the land, not out to sea.

We can travel by the stars. Doesn't matter how dark the
islands are, I can take a boat with a keel and no charts and go
wherever I need to go, all from navigating from the stars. I've
been with the sea for many, many years.

WASTE NOTHING

When we get the dugong, we don't waste dugong. Even the
turtle, the same thing, not even the bone. Every meat what's
on the dugong or turtle is shared, guts and all, everything.

Low tide mangroves, Badu Island

Share to everyone on the island. God gave that food for us to eat, not to waste. The dugong tail was for medicine or oil from the meat and fat, it was medicine. We had tuberculosis here during the war; a lot of people survived, because of that medicine. You can cook with that oil too.

You've got to keep following culture; when you keep out of culture, you will get in trouble. I hope the following generations after me will follow the culture. That's why we Elders keep that culture very strong for the younger generation to take part in, for their future. If they don't know then everything will be changed. You've got to show respect now for the world and everything in the world. The culture, that is the spirit of our forefathers; they are here. If you don't follow your culture, you're in trouble, you'll see what comes to you.

I'm sad about the commercial fishing, like trawlers, when they come they take all the fish out. We don't want them to damage all the seabeds. When they get a lot of fish they throw them back, but they're already dead; and when they go for crayfish there's nothing because the seabed is wrecked. That sea is the future welfare for us, it provides for us—not to be taken for granted, or be greedy with what it gives us.

BROTHERS AND SISTERS

We all have different struggles around the world, but if we all see each other as brothers and sisters and treat each other properly, like brothers and sisters, this world would be a better place. If you treat the lady next to you as if she were your sister, you will make sure you look after her good. If you look after her and make sure she has a good life and respect everything around her, we can all share and appreciate what this world has to offer. If we show more love and care for each other like brothers and sisters, the world will become good again. If you look at Indigenous culture it's about unity, not division; our culture is based on sharing and caring.

EPHRAIM BANI

I was first exposed to the wealth of the traditional knowledge in the 1950s through direct contact with my Uncles, the traditional teachers who taught me the ancient ways of survival, the recognition of spirituality and affiliation with nature.

By learning to understand the culture of the Indigenous inhabitant of Australia, it will encourage the growth of respect

Ephraim Bani

to the spirituality attached to it, which will trigger pride that one will find in its rightful place. 'Culture is a serious business and must be preserved for its perpetual continuality.'

There are two Indigenous languages and Creole lingua franca spoken in the Torres Strait. Lingua franca means universal language, it is used as inter-island language between the two languages of Eastern Island and Western Islands because they are otherwise unintelligible to both parties. Creole is used to communicate between. Creole was brought to the Torres Strait Islanders in the 1870s, originally from the Pacific Islands. It's a form of English with a word order of the traditional Torres Strait language.

The tools, food, materials and people correspond with the right environment, climate and geography. So all cultures are created differently to respond to their environment. It is by natural law that human instinct is stimulated to adapt to its surroundings; it is humans who create culture, shape traditions and practise customs. The social practices are customs, in these customs are stories, songs and beliefs which are handed down orally from one generation to the next to become what we call traditions. No one can judge a particular culture. How can a person from a completely different cultural background judge a culture alien to their way of living? Culture can be animated, assimilated, described and identified, but it cannot be evaluated except by people who have invented it.

All culture is something to be understood and respected. If it is treated disrespectfully, your chances of survival will be decreased. Culture enhances life and strengthens. It is therefore discourteous to criticise other ethnic differences. All cultures are god-given gifts for physical survival and spiritual awareness. Every one of us living under this heaven, no matter what colour, what creed, what language, what culture, are equal in status. It is important our culture and the languages be maintained so we can form a link to its origin, to our noble ancestors, to our islands and most of all to our paramount energy source, the beautiful blue waters of our Torres Strait. If we accept one another as equals and respect other cultural differences, we can breed love, which in time can blossom to peace among all that inhabit the Earth Mother.

We are so attached to what nature provided us, and in the early days our Elders would plant trees for our children and their children. The fruits will benefit them, and all the trees have meaning attached to them. To clear it to make modern things goes against our lore. If it needed to be cut, an Elder would have to come and talk to the tree. We do not just get rid of it, that's how big the attachment is. We have harvest ceremonies for the fruits that we eat. We have to talk to the trees—'Please bear for us so we can survive.'

COMMUNICATION

Telepathy is communication through mind power. There are some gifted people in the communities. Early people were able to communicate through minds from one place to another as if someone was whispering in your ear, but being so far apart. You can hear, not the voice, but what he or she is thinking at the place where the telepathy originates. The power of the unspoken word, it is mind to mind, and these are realities— spiritual connections.

Within the Torres Strait region, our forefathers navigated through the stars. They looked at the pattern of the stars in the sky. The stars even told them, 'Don't go tomorrow, the wind will be blowing too strong.' So it was nature's contact with the stars.

REPRESENTATION

We got our own flag in 1992. The government didn't see us as Torres Strait Islanders. We were all lumped up as Aboriginal, then just recently they identified the people as Aboriginal and Torres Strait Islanders. The colours of our flag: the blue represents the water and the sky; the green, the islands; and the black streaks represent the people; and the white headdress is our national symbol.

The flag for all Torres Strait Islands becomes a regional symbol for us. A separate people and culture in this region. We respect our Aboriginal brothers and sisters, our Papua neighbours too, but just to let the world know there are people living here that call themselves Torres Strait Islanders within Australia.

TOTEMS AND TATTOOS

The totem is the centre of Torres Strait traditions. It is one of the main elements that holds the societies together and operates law and order. The word totem originally comes from North American Indian language. It actually refers to animal or plant species that are held in special esteem by groups of individuals.

The sea

Totem is not a god or deity, as some perceive; nor is it an idol worship. Torres Strait has a group totem system of animals from the land, sea and air as well as edible totem plants.

We don't eat the totem except for communal meals, which are held once a year where we participate. I laugh at the idea where non-Indigenous say you have to go to the church to eat the communion, but we do the same thing. We had our own communions too—they say that is the demon's practice, but for me it is the same thing as having communion. We used tattoos to signify our totems, amongst other things. They were made from sharp fishbone and using the ink from a certain tree. Unlike our Aboriginal brothers and sisters, we did not practise body cuttings.

INITIATION

This story will avoid the forbidden and expose only the fundamentals of the whole subject. About thirteen or fourteen years of age, young females are held in seclusion for about a week from public view. This takes place when the young girl experiences her first sign of maturity. She is forbidden to touch anything or perform any household chores. During this time she is instructed by an elderly female called Ipika Maway who is her Aunt. Her basic instructions cover hygiene, childbearing, child delivery and the selected are introduced to the art of midwife.

Males of the same age too are called together and isolated from the village for about five to six weeks. The youths are called kernge, which can be interpreted today as 'candidate'. The youths can either come in groups or as an individual. Each kernge is taught by separate instructors, usually their Uncles. Kernge must learn to understand and recognise the flora and fauna, the local plant life, for their edible substance and medicinal value.

All this time he is placed on a special diet and taught the secrets of hunting methods and the skills to build or produce useful implements, such as digging sticks, the harpoon and so on. A special law is taught of the society and the recognition of the in-laws who call him Imi. He must now take a wife, learn to protect his family and provide for them. At night he is introduced to the heavens and its wonders. The stars are to predict the weather, and the travel of the constellations and the position of the solar system. The general expectation that is at the end of the initiation period, the kernge must become well familiarised with his environment in order to survive.

While the initiation is in full progress, it is the traditional law that the villagers must avoid the area at all costs, as the penalty for discovery is death. On each of the Torres Strait Islands a certain place was set aside called Kod. This was the place to be feared and respected, as this was where the traditional law was exercised. During the time of the initiation ceremony, the Kod dictates the tests of bravery, endurance of pain, and discipline. This was how reliable men and fierce warriors were produced. The kernge are placed prostrate on the ground, usually in the creek bed or some hollow place. The selected people wear masks to conceal their identities. In my home island of Mabuiag we have a place for this set aside.

These men whip the youths with dead coconut leaves set to fire. This is a test for endurance of pain and control of temper. The biggest test yet to come is shared by every kernge, the test of bravery where one must capture the biggest game from the sea, which is the dugong. When the initiation period is over, the kernge are painted after their totems and are rubbed by a sweet-smelling coconut oil. They are then led back to the village singing, as a feast is now in progress.

Both the initiated boys and girls now have a special place within the community. Both initiated are now fully aware of their totems, their kinship, their responsibilities and their social duties. They conform in obedience to moral conduct with enormous respect and appreciation to the social values of their community.

CONNECTIONS

One of the things that has saved our culture to this day is the water separating the islands; we can still practise our traditional fishing and family reunions and rituals. It doesn't matter that the missionaries came in. They stopped only what they could.

The crocodile in Torres Strait is a sacred creature as it is held in high esteem for its cultural value as a totem of most major clans. To escape if pursued on the dry land, one must be calm and avoid running on the muddy ground as the crocodile has the advantage to travel swifter by sliding on top of the mud. The best way to escape is to get to rocky grounds where the crocodile cannot sink its claws into the hard rocky grounds.

The crocodile possesses a long memory. When fishing on the coast we do not follow the same route regularly, particularly at dusk or at night when returning home from coastal fishing ventures. The crocodile marks its prey, recording the pattern of its movements. It naturally becomes the guardian and ruler of its habitat. Anything that falls into its territory becomes its subject or is otherwise challenged. So, very much like the crocodile, the Torres Strait Islanders and Aborigines or custodians of other world cultures have the natural ownership of their territory provided to them by trial and error, completing in a form of a blueprint that we label today as Culture. We are masters of our environment and are in full command of our survival.

THE ORACLE

In the Torres Strait the traditional senior Elders not only sustained themselves from energy sources yielded to them from land, sea and air. In fact they too tapped into the spiritual consciousness by forming an invisible link with the mysterious forces of the universe itself. The communication with Mother Nature was a serious business of survival. The acquired ability was transformed into a formula, later to be applied in a ritualistic form when recalled. An oracle is a respectfully constructed shrine with rocks, shells and animal bones and can be defined as a form of invisible communication. It can become a focal point to attract energy through Mother Nature in such a way that it can present a message to its consultant. However, this is not possible unless a ritual is performed.

In the early days our ancestors developed the hidden senses more fully due to survival. Our modern time gives us computers and calculators that we become so dependent upon that the machines become our masters, and that out of pure luxury we do not fully exercise our mind power and be available to our total self. So it does not matter what age, what era, we can still walk beside Mother Nature in rituals.

George Musgrave in song

CEREMONY & SONG

TAIPAN CLAN ○ **George Musgrave**

This land is Taipan Land, my land, my home. Taipan is our totem, can't touch him, even the emu and the red kangaroo, can't eat them one too, that's our story. See we pray for them, that's our story, same Taipan language, emu and red kangaroo. Taipans are on this land here now, don't go near him. You can only see him from a long way, he can see you too. Taipan is our people, we are Taipan clan. Other mobs can't come onto Taipan land, that's our land. Same as you white man way, you can't come onto my land unless you get permission from me. If I say no, you can't get in, that's the law.

Taipan language that's my language, that Taipan, me and my brother Tommy. I teach my grandchildren that language, I teach them bush tucker, bush medicine and trees in a language, my language from my Father, from olden days. I learn all that stuff from my Father and Grandfathers, they teach me all them things, like a bush medicine in case I get hurt. Even stuff that you rub on your feet, so you leave no tracks, I tried myself when I ran away from the station with that stuff. I dodged every police, I rubbed it on my feet and no one looked at me when I went with that medicine. I learn all them things from them old people, them olden-time Aboriginal people.

I'm on the dryland country, never go near the sea. Dry country a long way from the sea, dry country man Taipan. Only time our family went to the sea is when police came and took them away. We could have lost our language when the police sent our family away; people from this land are culturally dryland people, they were sent to Palm Island or Cairns on the coast.

TOTEM

The water eagle, the white-chested one, the fish eagle, that's what I become. I go into his body and fly with him, I work through the water eagle. My body in this chair here, no one touches me, they know I'm with the eagle. Everyone leaves me alone when I am like this. I can look down from the sky, I'm like a doctor man. My totem, that's the fish eagle.

MARRIAGE CEREMONY

The ceremony can be like the white people's ceremony: 'Are you going to look after her, will you bring food, treat her right way?' The man and the woman are both questioned, then a big dance, everybody dances. This woman is now Taipan and everybody says *yo* [yes], good, she'll be Taipan woman now. When I married my missus she became Taipan, and all the kids, even the grandchildren all Taipan. We can't turn them over, they're all Taipan.

You can't marry someone who is Taipan, because that's your full relation. You can't marry into your own country; you got to marry into a clan outside of your land. Even your cousin you can't marry, because that's the same language. If a Taipan man marry a woman from the coast, it won't be a coastal story [song ceremony], it will be a Taipan story. Because she married a

Early morning, Gulf country

Taipan, she'll become a Taipan woman. So if you choose to go to her land, it will be that story, her land story, everything is right this way.

SCARRING

The Taipan mark, the cut is like a tattoo, it represents our mob. Once that person is cut, no matter woman or man, they belong to the land, just like a bullocky's brand. When you get a body cut, we make them lay down and cut them. Then we put a charcoal on there, and get a little stick and tap hard and fast for a long time until the blood stops. Then we tap some more and talk Taipan [ceremony]; in the morning, all healed up.

We make the body cuts with the mussel shell, the one in the billabong, they're sharp. We do that cut to symbolise Taipan country. Taipan man cut across the top of the chest and the woman the same, three cuts, nicks, there above each breast, that's all. Some other place might chip the woman's hair off or put a nick on them another way. We don't do that, we just put a nick on the woman, above the breast, that's all. We knock out the tooth, man and woman. Tie a string around the tooth and pull it out, then a hot firestick on the gum, heals quick this way. Man fifteen or fourteen when cut, not too young.

When you go somewhere out of your country where there's other mobs who are cut or not, you know straight away 'you're black country man'; they will know you are Taipan. If you come into Taipan country with a clean skin or no mark on before, I look at you and think you might be a dangerous man with no mark, what will I do? I'll kill you.

THE BORA

Taipan have the Bora, the main area for ceremony for the man, more power there. You dance for might be five hours, then your Uncle comes up. I go then, he's going to dance in the Bora now until I come back again then. He's dressed up in full mud, same as you, you can only see his eyes. We won't dance for party, we dance for Bora power, spirit power. That Bora might go for days or might be weeks, but night-time we camp away from the Bora then. When you play Bora you're stripped naked, what they call *watakil*. And when he dances and bends down you can't laugh at him—no. If you fall by that, I mean laugh at him, you'll get set upon and the spirits will kill you, because you're not allowed to laugh when you play Bora, that's the law.

IN CEREMONY

We dance for the animal's spirit, become the animal in the dance, many dances, even dance about Aboriginal people and what they doing. One dance a woman sit down in the centre and the man dance around her until she becomes his sweetheart, this is a true story from my sister-in-law, we turn it into dance to show that story to them other mob. We had our Father and we had six brothers to teach us how to dance, how to sing in the Taipan language, and even in my missus' language too. We ran into a powerful Uncle to teach us in language and that's what we sing. Still today we play [corroboree], me and Tommy sing for all the young ones to dance now. I was taught song and ceremony by my Grandfather, traditionally really by him, my Grandfather Man. My Father asked his Father, 'How you getting along with your grandson?' 'I am learning him,' he said. Our Father said, 'Listen to what your Grandfather says.' We always go to the Grandfather for the teaching.

Tommy George, fire and spirit

TOMMY GEORGE

George Musgrave and me are brothers. I'm Taipan man too. I been married by promise, traditional way. No talking to the woman until you married, you don't go near her, father-in-law tribe is different tribe.

At the wedding the tribes make a fire, then my Grandmother and her Grandmother come up and talk to the girl. You wear dilly bag around the neck and across your back and have the dilly bag hanging behind you. Father-in-law touches you on the head with a woomera, and you can't see him coming. He can't talk with you, and that's where the law begins between us, that's the Murry Queensland Aboriginal way, you know. In the old days, you don't talk to the father-in-law.

The Grandmother comes up too, you don't see her coming, but you know what's going to happen, you got to. She's coming up behind you. You got to stand there, and if she sits down, then you right. One bloke over on the side hits the ground with a stick and makes a noise, right, you got it, that's the law, you going to get married now.

When you get married they make a fire for you both to camp there and get married and raise a family. That's our way, the old way. You know my Grandfather and Grandmother tell her what's going to happen, give her notice, you know. She was sixteen and I was twenty-one. I was supposed to marry a girl fourteen years old, Dad made arrangements and said no because she was too young.

SATISFYING THE SPIRITS

My traditional name is Woongarnum, it means to break or crack a bone. It's a lucky name connected to the spirits. We do warming [smoking] ceremony to satisfy and protect our people and to satisfy the spirits, that's an important one. When someone passes away, we smoke the ceremony, we get the bark from that kerosene bark tree and burn it with special leaves from a tree to make the smoke. We have to do this; it is the law.

As life goes on and changes, our dances change along with it. In my language what we call *butt-cha-kea* means corroboree, the dance. 'Come on, we'll go play corroboree,' I'd say, celebrate our culture through the stories in our dance. We started the Laura Dance Festival to show the world our culture. People came from all over the country to dance here. This used to happen in the olden days too, Aboriginal people come together from different [Australian] country to dance.

My tribe belonged to the way we paint our bodies. We paint our bodies from ochre or clay, we got places were we get it. Fifteen Mile Creek, that's where all the white clay there, white paint, my ancestors got it there, that's how I know.

AUTHOR'S NOTE

My first book, *Yolngu Mali* (Aboriginal Spirit), was a photographic story of seven months living in North-East Arnhem Land with the Gumatj clan of the Yolngu Nation. I went there in 1997 to produce black-and-white photographs that reflected the depth and completeness of traditional Indigenous culture, and to communicate the community's understanding of the importance of living in harmony with the natural environment. To help with this, I had equipment for developing and processing the images on location, which the Elders used to edit the photographs. By respecting the people's wishes and spending time with the community, the spirit of the culture itself directed the *Yolngu Mali* photographs.

In the making of *Yolngu Mali* I formed close relationships and learned from being part of a traditional community. It was important to settle into the community and not sit separate to anybody; to learn about clan totems and their significance, while embracing the different communities' homeland ways. These friendships and understandings, together with the assistance provided by the many Indigenous organisations and Elders Councils, enabled me to travel continuously for two years throughout Australia, visiting many communities to record their wisdom, for this book.

I witnessed the role of the Elders and the nature of the leadership they provide to their communities. The Elders are connected and bound by a highly evolved sense of culture and tradition; they see leadership as a responsibility, not a reward. This is in stark contrast to contemporary notions of leadership, which are focused on bidding for office on the basis of short-sighted policies rather than true leadership qualities.

Often Western society looks down on traditional cultures and knowledge, feeling superior as a result of science and enterprise, while ignoring the excessive, life-threatening costs that modern society and consumerism have imposed upon the world. With traditional knowledge and wisdom we can become aware of the connection between people, spirit and the earth, and, importantly, our reliance on this connection. There is much to be learned from the traditional owners of Australia, such as seeing ourselves as caretakers of the land and not its conquerors. The wisdom that Australian Indigenous leaders have to tell us has never been more relevant to us all than it is today.

PETER McCONCHIE

MAP OF ABORIGINAL AUSTRALIA

The map at right shows the general location of the 300-plus languages or nation groups of Indigenous Australia and the regions they belong to. These tribal/language groups consist of between 1 and 35 clans, each with its own dialect. The detailed maps on pages 114–15 focus on seven of the 18 regions within Australia and show the names of the tribal/language groups in the regions that the Elders interviewed for this book belong to.
Copies of the full version of this map which displays all individual language groups contained within these regions can be purchased from AIATSIS Sales, GPO Box 553, Canberra, ACT 2601.

DISCLAIMER NOTICE
This map indicates only the general location of larger groupings of people which may include smaller groups such as clans, dialects or individual languages within a group. Boundaries are not intended to be exact. For more information about the groups of people in a particular region contact the relevant land councils.

NOT SUITABLE FOR USE IN NATIVE TITLE AND OTHER LAND CLAIMS

D. R. Horton, AIATSIS, Canberra, ACT

Legend

RAINFOREST   Region name and boundary

Nakako   Tribal/language group name and boundary

No published information available

0   500   1000 km

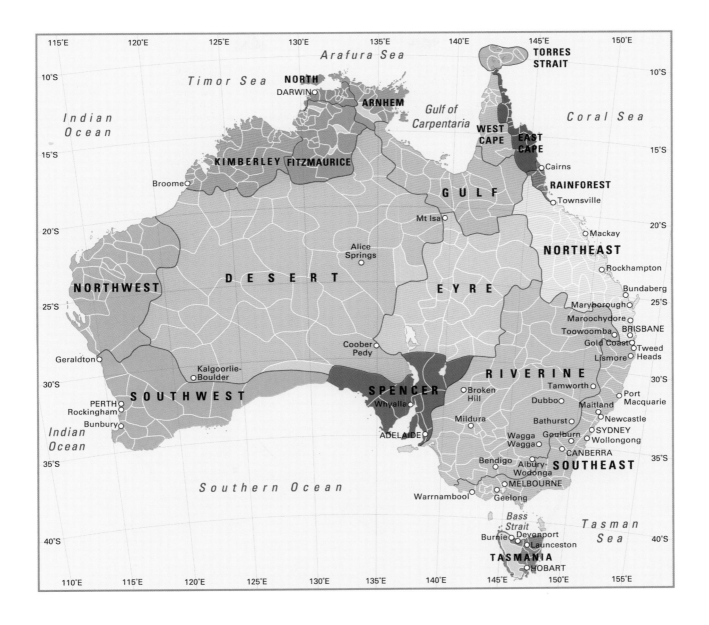

115°E 120°E 125°E 130°E 135°E 140°E 145°E 150°E

Arafura Sea

Timor Sea

10°S

NORTH

DARWIN

TORRES STRAIT

Indian Ocean

ARNHEM

Gulf of Carpentaria

Coral Sea

15°S

KIMBERLEY FITZMAURICE

WEST CAPE

EAST CAPE

Broome

Cairns

GULF

RAINFOREST

Townsville

Mt Isa

20°S

Alice Springs

NORTHEAST

Mackay

D E S E R T

E Y R E

Rockhampton

NORTHWEST

Bundaberg

25°S

Maryborough

Maroochydore

Toowoomba

BRISBANE

Geraldton

Coober Pedy

Gold Coast

Kalgoorlie-Boulder

Lismore

Tweed Heads

30°S

RIVERINE

SPENCER

Broken Hill

Tamworth

Port Macquarie

SOUTHWEST

Whyalla

Dubbo

Maitland

PERTH

Rockingham

Mildura

Bathurst

Newcastle

Bunbury

SYDNEY

ADELAIDE

Wagga Wagga

Goulburn

Wollongong

Indian Ocean

CANBERRA

35°S

Bendigo

Albury-Wodonga

SOUTHEAST

MELBOURNE

Southern Ocean

Warrnambool

Geelong

Bass Strait

Tasman Sea

40°S

Burnie

Devonport

Launceston

TASMANIA

HOBART

110°E 115°E 120°E 125°E 130°E 135°E 140°E 145°E 150°E 155°E

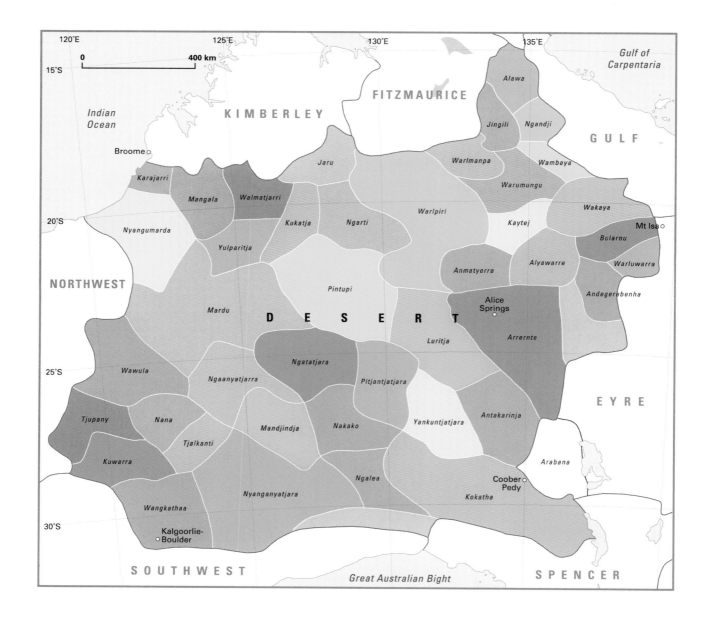

120°E   125°E   130°E   135°E

0   400 km

15°S

Indian Ocean

KIMBERLEY

FITZMAURICE

Gulf of Carpentaria

GULF

Alawa

Broome

Jaru

Karajarri

Jingili   *Ngandji*

Mangala   *Walmatjarri*

Warlmanpa   *Wambaya*

20°S

Nyangumarda

Kukatja   *Ngarti*

Warlpiri   *Warumungu*

Wakaya

Yulparitja

Kaytej   Mt Isa

Bularnu

NORTHWEST

Pintupi

Anmatyerre   *Alyawarre*   *Warluwarra*

Mardu

D E S E R T   Alice Springs   *Andegerebenha*

25°S

Wawula

Ngatatjara

Luritja   *Arrernte*

Ngaanyatjarra

Pitjantjatjara

EYRE

Tjupany   *Nana*

Mandjindja   *Nakako*   *Yankuntjatjara*   *Antakarinja*

Tjalkanti

Arabana

Kuwarra

Ngalea   Coober Pedy

Nyanganyatjara   *Kokatha*

Wangkathaa

30°S   Kalgoorlie-Boulder

SOUTHWEST   *Great Australian Bight*   SPENCER

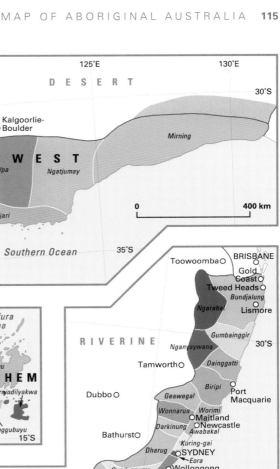

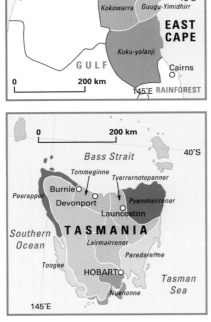